NIGHT SONG
SONGS OF REDEMPTION: BOOK ONE

Copyright © 2021, Daan Katz.
Second edition: February 2022

www.daankatz.com

NIGHT SONG

SONGS OF REDEMPTION
BOOK ONE

Companion to

NIGHT'S REIGN
CURSE OF THE FATHERS: BOOK ONE

Daan Katz

Contents

Preface

The beginning

Before the Beginning of Time,
an awareness began to stir in the midst of the Void.

The awareness grew and became God,
and God was everything, and God was nothing.
A being without substance, pure energy.

And God became two.

Male and Female, and they named themselves
Zinnir, He who watches,
and Oummi, She who hears.

They made their dwellings in Oummi's Vastness
and had seven children.

And their children created the worlds.

Part I

promise

night's reign
repels starlight
ghetto girl dies alone
another addict giving birth
to hope

14

vision

dragon
seeks sanctity
flickering flame kindles
tiniest spark illuminates
blind eyes

fever

hedgehog
grim harbinger
augurs mind-melting heat
dragonbreath quenches evil flames
and rules

highroad

guileless
hero takes flight
despised child remembers
rebel rises to challenge past
failures

secrets

thief yields
mighty dragon
limp knight shields lame warlord
combat master travels the world
beyond

obsessed

killer
prowls in darkness
dragon humbles giant
exile and tribe of lords unite
for life

locked in

early
despair relived
unsettles holy man
wheels turn to wrestle hidden truths
open

fated

daughter
of agony
heritage of heartbreak
ancestral perspective observes
the pledge

gloom's grip

substance
smothered by doubts
heir questions integrity
understanding shared in silence
restores

crisis

brutal
charges of guilt
spark violent thoughts of death
imprisonment brings rare comfort
from grief

manifest

hidden
key opens door
to darkness quelling aches
protector's skills cannot handle
lightly

flight

draken
wings sail into
endless days of summer
and futures unknown where pasts wilt
away

candid

anger
battles pity
as trouble roams the night
the tender opposes the strong
in love

pursuit

hidden
behind false names
they keep their secrets close
to their hearts as they fight against
whispers

27

fare

cautious
night time travel
shelters the innocent
where dragons' kin pursues her prey
and kills

alight

the flames
of hatred die
where sunshine brightens gloom
evil dies and nightmares are laid
to rest

hope

steadfast
against illness
and death the righteous stands
who from darkness brings forth child of
promise

hold

words fail
when dread provoked
by sovereign grasp induce
nightmarish visions of torture
and grief

ruin

lessons
in history
redouble sense of doom
crippling ancestral curse governs
ill minds

32

charge

exiled
and rejected
dragon defeats hunter
but surrenders to innocent
dreamer

foresight

erlen
king shares visions
of futures that might be
and cautions holy man to choose
wisely

alliance

dragon
shall rule again
as love brings unity
remnants of glory shall prosper
anew

Part II

marauder

hardened
man of rough seas
in search of the dragon
pained by resonance of magic
succumbs

38

recovery

dragon
master shelters
daughter of lost empire
rekindles flame of life inside
her soul

shaded

danger
prowls in darkness
ready to pounce and slay
heralds of dawn and favoured of
the gods

emergence

anger
rouses dragon
and reason dissipates
in scintillating clouds of hot
passion

uncharted

bereft
of kin and home
lost to their names they sail
into new beginnings and find
more grief

42

dedication

when breath
of life wavers
friendship is forged in stone
to safeguard mankind's destiny
from doom

obscure

guardian
of sleep comforts
deprived mourner seeking
heir amongst the lost deprived of
honour

star

bringer
of gloom dispersed
when sunrise wakes the day
and sorrow's child cleanses the house
of kings

rise

star shines
golden by night
staff and orb guide the hands
of him assigned to lead humble
mortals

inferno

lightning
strikes in dark night
brings fatal destruction
mournful memories mingle with
present

behold

dragon
eyes are swirling
blue and pink and golden
alive with memories of days
gone by

slayer

baleful
presence watches
passing through bounds of time
driven by thoughts of eternal
ruin

Part III

tangle

hated
for crimes his mind
can't remember his heart
yearns for redemption and healing
foretold

track

mountain
peaks high its path
hazardous and narrow
plunges pilgrims into deathly
defile

thrust

men scream
as flesh burns and
blood flows from fatal wounds
when the broken beat tyrant's trained
killers

reveal

golden
box enclosing
bittersweet memories
of budding love and shattered dreams
opens

annihilation

lethal
sickness unleashed
upon faultless victims
of slayer's voracious thirst for
power

restoration

past meets
present and life
moves towards new futures
where old sins are forgiven and
wounds healed

counting

pages
unspoilt by ink
denote new beginnings
and lessons to be learnt before
time's up

encumbered

courtly
obligations
clutter empty pockets
of time invading intimate
moments

sacrilege

past and
present collide
in nightmarish display
of contempt for decency and
honour

deluge

piercing
stare unsettles
sensitive awareness
till sight and sound and smell mingle
and strike

damage

blood like
crimson trail of
tears flows from innocent
victims' wounds despoiling sacred
substance

aftermath

wailing
shatters dead air
as young lives waste away
in stifling stench of somatic
discharge

Read Also

NIGHT'S REIGN
CURSE OF THE FATHERS: BOOK ONE

The grey stones of the temple had taken on a greenish hue, and the air smelled stale. Where were the candles? And why had the fountain gone dry? Surely, the gods had not forsaken this place? This was holy ground. Why was there no priest?

Time became a fluid thing as Shansi imagined herself back in Naz's strong arms. She clung to him as he held her and kept her from falling. His voice, warm and seductive as always, soothed her fears. The sweet scent of his skin comforted her. The luscious taste of his lips increased her longing for him.

Her excited moan turned into an agonised wail as pain shot through her abdomen again and forced her to her knees. Why could she not have been born a boy? In a reflex, her hand went to the medallion she wore on a delicate golden chain around her neck. Worth a fortune, yet utterly useless. If only she'd been able to sell it.

She rubbed the stupid tears from her eyes with the back of her hand, and forced herself to her feet. She had to be strong. For the child she was about to deliver into this world.

Please, good Goddess, I can't do this alone.

A faint noise, like a breath of wind, made her look up, and a beam of sunlight guided her eyes to the large statue. Gods be praised, it was still there and more magnificent than ever. As she set out towards it, another contraction made her double up on the floor again. Was this her punishment?

If only Baba hadn't gone missing. If only Naa hadn't died. And Mam. Asra and Siana. The useless tears came again. Shansi bit her lip. She sniffled. Wiped her eyes once more.

"Holy Gods! Be strong for once. Blazing. Be. Strong." She crawled closer to the statue of the Goddess, until finally she could touch it.

"Bring it on." Her voice sounded raw. Broken. Her womb cramped again. Hit by a bout of nausea, she swallowed the bile that rose in her throat. Her breath came in short, ragged bursts. A sudden cold made her shiver. Her legs started to tremble.

When the pain subsided, she tried to sit up, but almost immediately the next wave of pain crashed into her. In a vain attempt not to cry out, she dug her nails into her skin. Gods, but this was savage! How could any woman survive something as fierce as this? She closed her eyes. Bit her lip bloody. Dug her nails yet deeper into her skin. Gasped for breath.

*

For how long she lay there, on the cold stone floor, whimpering in agony, she couldn't tell. For once, there was no time. No hunger, no thirst. Not even the all-consuming need for a fix that had been the driving force behind almost all of her actions since little Siana died in her arms. If only she could have saved her sister.

If only she could have stayed with Naz. He had been good to her. He'd always provided her with the good, clean stuff. Not the rubbish on which she'd been surviving after she had left him. If only things had been different. If only his family could have approved. If only...

But all her if-onlies mattered not one bit. She was going to die today, and her child would become a retarded, sickly person. If it lived.

*

"Child."

Shansi opened her eyes and looked up. Someone was approaching. A woman.

"Are you..." Her voice cracked. "Are you the Goddess?"

"No, child." The woman came closer. "Just her servant. I was sent to attend to your needs. Drink some." She supported Shansi as she offered her a small cup of water. Then she wiped her face with a cool, damp cloth. "Is that better?"

Shansi nodded. It wasn't much. A shot of Saffire Tease, or even Hog Flare would have been considerably better, but that was not an option. She had to think about her baby. In all honesty, she should have been doing that since the day she discovered she was with child, but she'd been too selfish.

More contractions. More pain, ever more unbearable. The nausea came back with such force she threw up. Another shiver ran down her spine. Her legs started trembling anew, and worse than before. She grasped at her swollen belly, writhing. A suffocated wail escaped from her lips.

The woman stayed by her side and tried to make her as comfortable as possible. Though it brought little relief, it was still better than having to go through this nightmare alone.

Just when she thought she couldn't take it any more, her baby was born. A beautiful boy with golden eyes and copper skin. Just like his father.

She must have lost consciousness then, because next she woke up in a real bed, between soft silken sheets, in a cool, well-ventilated room. The lady from the abandoned temple sat on a chair beside her. The child, her child, lay in a basket.

"My son..." She barely had the strength to whisper. "Is he... is he...?" She couldn't bear to finish the question. She knew the answer already. He would die and she, his own mother, was to blame.

"He is weak, but I'm confident that he will pull through. I gave him the medallion. It will give him the strength he needs. Was it your father's?"

She shook her head. "My grandfather's. His wife and other children died from the pestilence. Long before I was born. My mam..." She closed her eyes. So tired. Even just breathing took almost too much effort. "Mam was his only remaining child. But she's dead too, now. They all are."

"I see. I'm sorry." The woman was silent for a moment, then asked, "What will your son's name be, dear?"

"Moradin." It had been Naa's name, and it seemed fitting that her son should be named after him. "Can I..." The nausea found her again and made her cut off her words. She shivered with cold. Black specks swam in front of her eyes.

"Child!" The woman stood bent over her, felt her forehead, her pulse. "Stay with me, girl. Stay with me!"

"Cold," she said through chattering teeth. "Naz." She grew colder still, and weaker. "Naz..."

Naz took her in his arms. "Don't be afraid." His body felt warm against hers, and his voice sounded more alluring than ever. "Nothing will hurt you."

"No!" a woman's voice cried out in the distance. "Don't you die on me. Don't..."

About the author

Daan Katz was born in 1963 in The Hague, the Netherlands, where he also spent the first fifteen years of his life.

From a very young age, Daan has been enchanted by stories. When immersed in his books, Daan would forget everything else. The real world would cease to exist, and there was only the imaginary world, with his imaginary friends, who would continue to speak to him long after he'd finished reading the book.

Given his love for stories, it was only natural for him to start writing his own as soon as he realised that he could. From there, poetry was a logical next step.

Connect with Daan on Facebook or Instagram, or via his website.

https://www.facebook.com/DaanKatzAuthor
https://www.instagram.com/katzdaan
https://daankatz.com

Sign up for Daan's newsletter and receive a new short story every month.

https://daankatz.com/newsletter